SONGS THAT REMIND US OF FACTORIES

Songs That Remind Us of Factories

Danny Jacobs

NIGHTWOOD EDITIONS

2013

Nightwood Editions
P.O. Box 1779
Gibsons, BC von 1vo
Canada
www.nightwoodeditions.com

THE CANADA COUNCIL | LE CONSEIL DES ARTS
FOR THE ARTS | DU CANADA
SINCE 1957 | DEPUIS 1957

BRITISH
COLUMBIA
ARTS COUNCIL
Supported by the Province of British Columbia

Nightwood Editions acknowledges financial support from the Government of Canada through the Canada Book Fund and the Canada Council for the Arts, and from the Province of British Columbia through the British Columbia Arts Council and the Book Publisher's Tax Credit.

This book has been produced on 100% post-consumer recycled, ancient-forest-free paper, processed chlorine-free and printed with vegetable-based dyes.

TYPESETTING: Carleton Wilson
COVER DESIGN: Jesse Jacobs

Printed and bound in Canada.

LIBRARY AND ARCHIVES CANADA CATALOGUING IN PUBLICATION

Jacobs, Danny, 1983–, author
Songs that remind us of factories / Danny Jacobs.

Poems.
ISBN 978-0-88971-292-8 (pbk.)

I. Title.

PS8619.A254S65 2013   C811'.6   C2013-903345-9

ACKNOWLEDGEMENTS

Some of these poems first appeared in the following journals: *The Antigonish Review*, *Arc*, *CV2*, *Event*, *The Fiddlehead*, *Grain*, *The Malahat Review* and *Riddle Fence*. Many thanks to the editors of these publications.

"How to Shoot Skeet with My Grandfather's Lost Double Barrel" placed first in *Grain*'s 2009 Short Grain Contest.

I gratefully acknowledge the support of the Nova Scotia Department of Communities, Culture and Heritage, who provided financial funding during the writing of this book.

Thanks to Silas White and everyone at Nightwood Editions who helped make my book a much better one.

To Brian Bartlett, Mark Jarman and Ross Leckie: thanks for the notes, remarks and marginalia. Great teachers, all.

Thank you to Jesse Jacobs for drawing the cover image. And thanks to my parents for their love and support throughout the years.

"Days" is for Great Shea.

Finally, love and gratitude to Sarah for her patience and encouragement. Without you there wouldn't be a book.

CONTENTS

Troubling States

Wrap Time

PIPELINE

Through the thaw my godfather worked the pipeline,
trenched clear-cut biomes with the cupped hand ·
of a digger, laid a shunt through the flawed
heart of northern scrubland, wrenched gears

from the cab while boom and dipper coughed
through trough and aquifer, was told he'd die
if he didn't get his shit together—
his heart hydraulic, trackdrive and torque.

That winter he quit hard liquor and cut down
on smokes, cut the blue rind of foot-deep
dawn snowdrifts on walks with sister-in-law.
When she stayed home he'd go it alone.

But so much for the grading, the levelling
for even ground; in the end not some crossed-
signal in the cells that did it but the quick physics
of skid and drift: a road, sun catching on chrome.

EXCAVATOR DREAMS

In every cratered and dream-dead lot,
corroded excavators dream hydraulic
among the untouched musculature of tract
housing. In their carapace of dream, blown
ichor sluices through hose and tube to move
blocks gouged from strata and seam; crumbled
marl hefted in noiseless dream, cupped buckets
lifting trinkets from just-dug dreams: a locket
fused shut from a stubborn lock dream, clothes caught
on roots from coital fever dreams, the light
bulb of a fox kid's skull holding hare's fear
dreams, the dream of the driver grinding gears,
ragweed pollen catching morning beams
in the cuboid void of the recurring quarried dream.

LIGHTNING RODS

Look: they came with the place,
roof's half-assed shot at Gothic,
bent spikes riding the arch of it,
wires spidered on eave and gable
to ground volts til the maple
roots jerk in their soil. Suspect
if ever they caught sky's lit wick,
charmed cloud to mossy shingle.

Before the walls get bulldozed
and the beams fall in, my uncles
and I might straddle the ridge,
grab lengths of rebar and hope
for storms—the copper funnels
of our spines fine-tuned conduits.

LAWN BOY

Left out through winters,
you're the goofy dude, scrawny
dud, caught with dated paint
job and cuckolded by

Yard Men, ride-ons, brawny
showstoppers that can rock
an acre with twenty-four horses,
those six-speed jocks, all cock.

Praise God or get a grimoire,
deities need conjuring
to get a retort from your ripcord.
Shin-high grass at the siding

but your motor's furrows
hold a botched or locked-in
flake of steel stalling the mow,
a splinter in the engine's skin.

I'll play necromancer
of bolts and two-strokes,
show your humours, divine answers
from jury-rigged striped screws

shucking their rusted crusts
like chrysalises—your dried-out
innards laid out on oilcloth
some garage-floor tarot.

Something here about hope
for the underdog; buck up:
you're old-school, cousin
of the scythe, tetanus-giver

who mulched three decades
without a stall, cutting through
the dreams of Sunday drunks.
You're us at one time or another:

wracked by stillness, nostalgic,
awry, colicky for motion
and push. When remade,
may you, graceless throwback,

shake off your misgivings, miss
all field mice and hack swaths
with lichened blade through
my first, my shoddy lawn.

WEEDING

Quackgrass, curly dock, nutsedge,
nimblewill. Ragweed, smartweed,
pigweed, yarrow. Each oval
under tree a topiary of weed.
Between esteemed perennials
a copse of sprig and spiked leaf
jostle for elbow room: lowbrow
garden thugs loud-talking lupins,
busy-handed nutrient filchers,
Darwin's ubiquitous trench-coat creep.
I could bust up the pest party, spray,
strapped in, tanked toxic slosh.
Or get my hands dirty, go old-school,
herbicidal maniac, break my back,
tug and twist til the cows come home,
pull my wrist while pulling loose
a clutch of crabgrass from its death
grip on soil, roots muscled hands
that'll be damned before they give.
Even with the tempered rubber
the *Tough Guy* work gloves can't
brook it: each weed pulled's
another bur in my thumb's
soft meat. Truth: I'd rather leave it
to chaos, nature's oddball math;
why try drunk punching through
a losing brawl? No matter what I do,
they'll stay on for the extinction,
still ripe for blooming after
we're gone, weaving rib cages
to dreamcatchers, our eye sockets
small clay pots for dandelions.

YARD WORK

One of those call-in-the-counsellors crashes—
one dead, the teen driver cane-bound, left home
manning the leaf-blower. Their backyard a clutch
of landfill tonnage, what their field won't give up—

upturned hands of pronged farm gear. Chisel plow,
spike harrow. A herd of blocked John Deeres,
transmissions bracken full and sheathed in fern.
The above-ground pool a cyst of leaf-thick rainwater.

All's a backlog of rust keeping pace with accident.
Or perhaps jumble's par for the course, the lawn lax
before the mishap; perhaps we're held sightless
in the rat trap of cause and effect, ignoring facts—

that the lot's always been a perpetual
going-to-seed, slow seepage over the property line.

SEED SONG
for Sarah

The pulp, the mash:
sliver and wedge
brown like old prints

and our fingers lock
in glass bowls,
the cores' husks

scraping our hands.
When I left you kept
a seed—a finch's heart

tucked in sod—
and sang to it,
citing cell science,

the need for vibration,
how a voice
can help lay down

roots, braid the soil,
grow the shaky
beginnings of a tree.

OX

In my city boy blunder I called it bull,
ducked its stare and deemed it rash, riled,
boiler tank of thrust, hatchback-sized flexed
bicep set to charge the sagged cats' cradle
of rusted wire, go gorge happy and play
longhorn sky-high ragdoll before we
snap a single profile pic. But haughty
me, its eyes all opacity and ennui:
a glance that judged us rubberneckers,
upright dolts, assured its recast status
of withdrawn workhorse beyond all bluster
and slow with loss. We might've been
blackflies, bluebottles, tuneless bother
breaking vigil for its late yoke brother.

POTATOES

Plump geezer mugs, grubby monks,
  cosmic eggs for dirt universes,
there's tired wisdom in your waiting—

hushed dust doldrums before hands
  go medieval, plop you in pots,
bifurcate your calm lumped bodies

and salt the post-op. Shrewd tuber
  used to sacrifice, lord knows
you'd rather save a famine than

get shoved up a pipe's greased anus
  so drunk hobbyists can hope for
yardage, launch your ovoid corpus

through the suburbs. Rooted hermits,
  selfless stems stretching sprouts
through the mesh of sack, stay put,

feed us, pray for rebirth while dozing,
  while you flower third eyes, new
light hairlining the cupboard's crack.

BARGAIN BIN

The whitewashed drywall woke as BiWay
and I, nigh on eight, decried the toy display's
lack of good Lego, all knockoffs and Duplo.
By grade five she was re-signed and sold to
Woolco, this before a brief stint as SAAN—
weak real estate's circadian rhythm,
same shit different aisle, bins of Bugle
Boy and bungee-roped rubber balls, back stock
unboxed and marked for blowouts. While frugal
ladies lollygagged and haggled, made slapdash
muzak in the key of jangled hanger,
in walked the new century to sweet talk
the walls into fishnets of fibre-op,
row the floor with chain gangs of chopped desktop
Dells. Before long we're in for the long haul,
twitchy phone pitch wizards picking foam
from levered ergo-thrones. A banner snaps
epileptic in the parking lot squall,
screams *Join the Team*; they're roping in
hopefuls with a flair for the upsell. We'll
bid on hours and carpool to the nightshift,
parse new mall smell from dying mall smell.
The food court's robot, once ridden for
a quarter, is just not ridden anymore.

SCRIPTED PITCH

It's good to ditch it before you're spent,
gone ga ga, lost in the bilge and spillage
of millions, digits hardly sifted then
fixed in the remixed rhythm of algorithm,
the dialler's quick-handed magic trick.
Within these grey walls of pinned-up
buzzwords nothing's analog, you're licked
before the call comes kicking in, stuck
retching out rebuttal, calming this Texan
and his conniption fit. This, while new
dupes are queued in the bionic lexicon
of whirring servers, wait to be spewed
to the cursed few cursing the split shift,
styed eyes and mice scrolling styleless script.

Insight.

If you leave for home with your headset
still horseshoeing your neck like a sci-fi ascot,
keep it in a pencil-punctured shoebox with a nest
of woven modems; feed it touchtone erratics,
learn to coo in phreak and static.

Two rebuttals for each call. They will love
you on each call. When wrapping
calls reflect on all they have given,
and likewise what you have given. Become
the customer in pacing and slang. Oblige them

despite their thoughts on our winters. Pens
are contraband in the paperless environment.
Remove family pictures at the end
of each shift. If wait times between calls are long,
study up, learn the mnemonics,

there's tips on our Intranet. See us as we are,
see us up to speed with ISO 9001.
Check the manual: the CSR's Necronomicon.
Don't dither if the mark gets mouthy; be Zen—
they've been called and will be again.

The Do Not Call List does not exist.

Innovation.

Pick us, Capital One, our agents
can fake it—

they practise accents
and acronym

their call-back comments
to cut down

on off-call minutes,
use pseudonyms

if their names are a bit left
of Western. Test them—

our training's long and useful—
we fulfill

Your Clientship's want list
with group games

like the one where they draft
the ideal rep on newsprint.

Bathroom time is logged (seven minutes a shift)
but mistake us not,

we're hardly tyrants: we fan
a full house of scratch tickets,

say *Take your pick!*
Our Performance Excellence

Procedures have outperformed
our competition

in every metric of Performance
Procedure Evaluation.

Our hardware drones with the bones
of small watches.

We're eager for keeners
and will interview walk-ins,

our banks of servers
are peregrine falcons.

Imagination.

Font coiffed
to an Apple product gloss,
set in 700 pt., catchwords
culled from the mission
copy and tactically plastered
on the call floor columns' midriffs,
wall text set to explicate
the conceptual
art of the cold call. Nouveau
Blue on Space Slate Grey—
feng shui of the latter day.
Phrases ripped from framed
boardroom landscape bumph,
but blown, full stops
the size of plates.
Each i-word's got clout
with its own period
and tops the corporate letterhead.
Designed by the top dog
at the firm that did Asurion, ICT,
like most things in the vicinity,
it's assured, minimal,
to the millimetre,
not quite subliminal
but of the skin of the place.
Soft-spoken business casual,
idiom personified
as the boring guy
beside you
at the interview.
To each hardened
CSR body rocked

by the claymore of a Monday,
they're word as surface,
background décor—signified
an outsized suit the signifier
lost. Yet watch
the sapped trainee
scan each, pushed to try,
to take something
from nothing.
Insight. Innovation.

Imagination: pre-
recorded android voiceover
pinging in a neocortex
fold—*When confronted*
with what to wear,
remember
good choices can be made
with a dressier sandal.

Tell Macarius the Elder, tell Euthymius
the Younger, tell Benignus, Alphege,
Donnán, and Egwin: we got nothing
for punchy PR stunts. Our slickest staff
are trying their best just to hold up
the big guns. They may bitch we're bureaucrats,
God-lit pencil pushers, but relate
the logistics—we're losing millions
and need to back our first stringers,
the go-to guys from Sunday school,
deep-eyed regulars still showing up
for death throes and burnt toast.
We know Almachius chucked himself
among a gladiatorial muck up in Rome
but our numbers are low and it's hardly
the time to push the unknowns. Sure some
pulled their one-time dime-store wonder, but
a chunk of those loners, those lacklustre
cave-dwellers, are phony brown-nosers,
dusty bores with postcard hagiographies.
Stoned to death? Found a monastery
in Passau? So? Little meat for our
conglomerate. Don't sugar-coat it,
we need old hands to get back the cynics:
dragon slayers and haloed stigmatics,
not weak-kneed ascetics. Half our team's
gone New Age and we'll be damned before
we tout some worn scribe from the asshole
of Constantinople. In a word, they should
shut it, grab a vision when they can, and
leave the heavy lifting to the in crowd.

They're just like our dumbstruck carbon
jokes down below, always pleading, *Look
at us, our tricks. We need to be loved.*

PAID TRAINING

A shift of paltry rewards. We're all half-
there, all somnambulant and getting bold
with the dress code. No jeans or spaghetti straps,
we're told; no backtalk during PowerPoints.

This summer we'll do the circuit, hit all
the hub's malls razed for telecom, three weeks
then gone, each building architecture's dull
Xerox, each crop of newbies zonked by first break,

relearning boredom as solid-state physics,
some condensed dim aspic hard to talk through
when TLS harp on the client's bugaboos—
high AHTS with low ASAS don't mix,

we're gunning for goof-offs with weak KPIS
so don't expect incentives with slack wrap times.

ON BREAK

Joggers pace the parking lot
decked in Gore-Tex,
reflector strips
in flux:

slow strobes
flashing to the suburbs,

fanned in mist, bereft, and lost
umbrellaless. Wet
spectres licked
with lux,

tuned low
to rain's static curbside.

A FIFTH FACTORY
after Karen Solie

Dredge outlying streams, the Chocolate River;
everything's fine, to code. But remain on
edge for the spill you can't see, invisible
pollutants rounding the hub of Moncton,
angry voices ringing off-time in low
hum, sinusoid. Press up against the din,
don a headset—there's something below
hearing that rattles the junked violin
of your rib cage, static pulse passed tuning,
signal-crossed, noise gorged on binary,
full to silence, two hundred voices calling
inbound, wave functions breaking the levy
of their equations. Inside, they sit askance,
ceiling fans in tandem with the resonance.

Click

DOMESTIC ENTOMOLOGY

i. Chalybion californicum

One look
then that getimoff
getimoff flinch.
B-movie walk-on
stunned by your own iridescent
illusive blue—
quick flash
of spacecraft turtle wax.
Stuck dive-
bombing kitchen windows,
you're half Porsche, half
buck wagon
dragging
the heavy reins
of your back legs.
O spindly gaggle of sticks,
o gangly wicket, o cerulean jewel,
o robo-drone,
go back
to your overlords,
we may mean you harm.

ii. Drosophila melanogaster

Slave to ferment,
          metaphor for every sot and juicer
ignoring the drowning risks, you bounce
from blueberry
          to peach pit
               chasing the dragon
of your first rot hit.
          Brain box stopped-
up with the musk of week-old plums, you'll do
          dust mote jazz over
a wineglass lip, the last party
          drunk slamming the butts of empties and
               calling out,
to no one, for more.
          Despite our harsh laws on compost,
          we know you're legion,
Fifth Horseman of the Apocalypse, cloud
          scourge sketching
        saccadic infinities above
the day after silt of lined beer bottles.
          Through our hangovers,
          a note from the other side
warning that death gets in
          the smallest of cracks.
Noiselessness ringing, saying *give in, give in.*

iii. Forficula auricularia

Come out from drains
and the puckered noses
of the dead. Warn us
to shake out our shirts.

Teach us the nightmares of children,
the Triassic, the space between
counters, motel carpets.
     Fan of the liminal,
we found you walking the scummed
gap between sink
and backsplash, the fridge door's pleated seal.

More Kafkaesque than Nabokovian,
you're jealous of the butterfly.

Like the fat kid with the funny name,
your reputation precedes you
and is wholly unfounded. Against
my better nature, I'll always
go for the kill—break you
in the white rose of crumpled tissue.

Desperate for comrades you worship
the vice-grips, the BBQ tongs.
Come closer, you say. *I won't bite.*

iv. Musca domestica

Buzz-drunk zealots, one-track
ascetics dying at the foot
of the ledge; not knowing glass,
you give your life to screen:

that all-seeing compound eye
of your warped bug god
flaunting the infinite outside.
Beyond all walls, you're sure

all's cowflop, raw meat, the red
jewellery of opened roadkill,
a free-for-all suck-and-gorge
with your brothers in blight.

Once let out, resplendent,
from this living room prison,
choose kill-sites wisely:
you have two weeks.

v. *Larinioides cornutus*

You seem to say: *Game of chess?* Or:
You'll blink first. On slow days
you fuss with differential equations
and debunk myths about the weather.
Your back's fractalled, the dashed-off
efforts of Mensa brats, nature's stab
at the Julia set. At dinner parties
you recite whole passages of Euclid's
Elements. During downpours, you leave
your body for the astral plane but
have no time for the occult.
Connoisseur of stillness, while rolling
a catch it's all whirling dervish,
blue-ribbon basket-weaver, frumpy
maid working the washboard, thin-
armed composer nailing the theremin
section from the *Requiem Aranea.*
Dewdropped architect, calm schemer,
I'd rather let you be than drown in rain.

vi. Anax junius

Kin of cross and skeleton key.
Gatekeeper, day sleeper, rune
carved on dug up Hopi bowls,
your guard at the doorframe lasts
all morning. As if there's hope
to die in sleep then rise
as ornate doorbell, filigreed and
inset with emerald. Hard not
to see you as omen, wings
spread to augur: *Watch out*
for erratic drivers, falling
tree limbs. Expect a phone call.

Swamp swizzle stick, eye extractor,
every time I entered I expected
a hum behind my shoulder.
You'd darn my lids shut
while I dream your ancestors:
raven-sized spy planes picking
off tetrapods through oxygen
stuffed bog land. But the next day
you'd left to waylay blackflies.
I'll miss your gemstone carapace,
the change to the décor, but I'm free,
unharmed, and glad you're gone.

vii. Culex pipiens

Despot phlebotomist,
pathogen change purse,
you snub the rare sting,
the sporadic way feeble
bees swell the tongues
of clumsy Frisbee-golfers.
No, you think macro: diseased
townships. In dark rooms,
you plan the next pandemic,
quaff Cab Sauv and ink
countries in red on maps.
Bollocks to black widows,
bullet ants, there's grander
ways to fell a mammal.
Jumpy with bloodlust,
you're not averse to the quick
guzzle, the unplanned chug:
somewhere, a passed out
camper sleeps one off while
ten of you sip the vein-thick
outcrop of their one shoeless
foot. Shoddy sommelier plump
with another's AB, I'm up
half the night tuned to your
frequency: high whir going
Doppler over our ears, sine-
waving the walls of our bedroom,
dowsing the dark for platelet
rich groundwater, the perfect
place to enter and kiss.

viii. Gryllus pennsylvanicus

The rains came
and we let the back go
pasture, a half-acre knot
of unwashed hair. Beneath
a whorl of interlocking
weed you held court, knocked off
trills while we slept, turned backyard
to amphitheatre. One night I stood
end-stopped at the field's edge
stunned by your stridulation,
the undergrowth giving up
a surge of chirp, a ring
tuning the back of my jaw. I could part
the brush all night without
tracking one note back to an owner.

Obsidian sliver, cornstalk fiddle,
you prefer a wobbly dirge on handsaw
to symphony, you own the meadow
but choose to die belly up
in the bottom of Crock-Pots. It's past midnight
and we've drank to you;
play us out on the rough cut diamond of your wings.

ix. Trojan Horse

We dolled out snake oil to the workers,
unscented street gin they lapped
ten to a drop—mascara-gooped
eyelashes circling the beaded eye of Ant-B-Gon,
gaster gorgers fat with nanolitres
for the colony's thirst-wracked hive-mind.
　　While sloughing dollops
to the chaos, I thought pine horse or PC virus,
thought forbidden fruit, poison wells,
peer pressure, bear traps, chicken piccata
hot with a scrum of E. coli, the way we're duped
and bent double with want or the wrong food;
　　　　in the face of their pester,
I aped guilt and dreamt genocide
for our sleight of hand, the spiked sugar water
brought wide-eyed to the foot of the queen.

x. Swatter

Swiftly whipsnap
the crud buzzing
bastards after
they two-step
your cookie, mack
on the chucked
pork chops' grey
rot, slobber on
trashbound corn
cobs, lay eggs in
the wet slits of
tainted t-bone,
wring palms like
two-bit used car
hawkers over
dried ponds of
chicken froth;
be kung-fu quick,
become one with
the business end's
flat porous hand,
chant kill with
each wrist flick,
go ape shit with
your implement
but be cool in
the backswing.

xi. Panopticon

I emptied the dregs of a cheap red to bring them in, a thimbleful
haunting the bottom of a saran-topped goblet's broad bowl.
Within a morning, dozens fought the wine's stick, heady
with tannic haze: a mean bouquet. Nuts with want, they
crawled through the polyethylene holes and found Phlegethon
while I watched, a vengeful God, from my spot atop the panopticon.

BETTY GOODWIN SOUND INSTALLATION

Dalhousie Art Gallery, 2010

Struck dumb, spooked
with a tincture of pitch,
a jumbled crumb
of shush stuck in
in sieve of my eardrum.

What I'm hearing is speech
gone wonky, phonetic trill
washed to phoneme,
all plosive and fricative,
the quiet click of small

things: change worried
in pockets, a man down
a well humming
quadrilles, linen pulled
through a napkin ring.

This is how sound works;
like everything else
a play of atoms.
From the desk its tremor
attempts language—a shadow

of throat-song. I get up
to find the source; but close up
another dull occurrence
of art and context,
speaker-wrapped sculpture
and the gab of spoken tripe:

The silence must go on   can't

Encased and safe: my white Siberian tiger-down parka sloughs the sweat with a Mayan codex lining. I breathe slow; this Amazon air clears the lungs: nightshade and passion fruit pumped from two hundred mason jars under the hood, powdering my Saharan cypress dash with the dust of zodiac moths. Detour for a double-double. I spin twenty-four-inch rims forged from sarcophagus gold, onyx inlay, Grecian shards. I turn the volume knob—a ring copped from an Aztec cleric. The chic speakers pump surround-sound tribal throb on tama and djembe as I groove with coffee, complain away the cold. Palming gibbon-skull gearshift, I peel through suburban shortcuts and trail two femmes walking tea-cup poodles, roll down medieval glass windows, tilt shades dyed eagle aqueous humour, hitch up my Oaxacan coral snakeskin tie, and smile an honest smile.

TOME

Hantsport, Nova Scotia

Giddy with the Carboniferous, I huff up
the bluff's pitch with a ten-pound slab
just pinched from Blue Beach: sheaves
of pressure-stamped era
collated from the Book of Lith,
straight-cut rhombus sheared off
from nature's packed-
down lees. Rock's biopsy sample,
deep-time casserole, inch-thick glued-shut
hardback from some bygone zoic.
Plumb enough to upright on bookshelves,
each waterlogged page is a thousand years
of coal swamp, river dreg; one black-rimmed
hair's width the pressed leaf
of a generation's bad weather. Tucked somewhere
between sandstone and shale, a love letter
to the Law of Superposition:
a single footprint from a flathead tetrapod
scouting the Late Devonian, tube sock of axons
taunting gravity with a new backbone,
calling us back to mornings
when we half wake, still slaves to
hindbrain, to stretch our spines, sniff the air.

DESIGN NO. 101—SPECIFICATIONS OF AN AUXILIARY KETCH YACHT

Lines found in William J. Roué Fonds, Dalhousie University Archives

Laying Down

The yacht to be properly
laid off, full size on
the mould loft floor; care
taken that she is properly fair
and sweet from all angles.

Workmanship

All timber to be sound, free
from bad knots, shakes and defects.
Outside planting to be caulked
with best cotton
and fire thread oakum.

Painting

A gold line to be worked around in cove
out in sheer strake with gold leaf.

Great. Another straight-faced romp in cliché. I'd give transom and
    taffrail
to deter more showy poets obdurate in slogging out Maritime
    doggerel

for self-dashed chapbooks. Sure, my strut-sagged keel bears
    likeness
to the rummy guts of fishermen granddads but I sure as shit won't
    miss

another ode couched close to solipsistic sonnets on lobster traps
    and gannets.
I'm done in, stuck fast on the mud banks of the Avon; why care I
    of stanzas

relating fateful jaunts with deckhands? First off, it's a crock and
    recidivist
when chumps pen one-offs about bottomed-out trawlers. Spastic
    fake lyricist,

get to the gist of this, I'll look folk for the photo-op but for the
    couplets
do me a solid: tow me to the brink and sink me for a guiltless

death at sea lest I'm blind-sided and caught sepia on some GG
    nominee.

THREE FRAGMENTS TO HER HAND

I

Her hand over
piano keys

a breaker of vein
riding deeper
currents of bone.

II

Her fevered body all tube and fissure—

hand a wheat spikelet
lost among hillocks of pillow.

III

The hand in sleep: seashell made sleek
by the pull of waves and sheet.

ICU

Sore-backed nannies chase
the mess of them caught
with plastic blocks
and Cabbage Patch Kids,
the faces caved in.

Parents bump off
reception desks like cephalopods,

aimless with fret, the underbrush
of a thought—
        misplaced
cells the body calls out,

murk of flesh
                weaving the body's trellis. Just that.
And no,
        we shouldn't be here:

echoed place where the day's shrunk
        to a dirge of sighed cusses,

where the rooms are white,
                                stop-timed
like the dream of a boy running.

CACOPHONY

or dive-bomb caw and cheep
melee twitterpated with day,
sponge-boned polyglots
catcalling mates,
birdbrain word-horde
sure to trip up part-time ornithophiles
trying to match each trill and buzzsaw squawk
to a species. This creak and whirr
likely heard when a synesthete sees
a Kandinsky—songs
that remind us of factories.
One's doing phlegm
roped smoker, one's doing squeaky
swing set—the front maple
noise machine's not charm or kettle,
murder or wisp, but melting pot
shrieking *wakey wakey* straight
from the syrinx: atonal argot
in lingua Aves, my morning
dream of too much talk,
of feckless flight then falling.

Troubling States

HOBBYIST

Tinkerer, tool-gopher, belt-buckle beer cracker—
my neighbour builds the Bomb,
jury-rigged Little Boy,
frumpy bolted hulk with breech plug,
lift lug, and locknut flush to the inch.

With wife gone he shunned his lawn
and got stuck on mock-ups. Wind-snug,
dud draft plans hugged my screen door all spring
like dinner invitations from the desperate.

    He told me once
that gun method fission's a kind of love-making,
white-snap coupling in the bomb's hull,
uranium ring fired to its phallic mate—
yonic cup, ionic yawn.
And then snow, or something like it.

Funny how a box of light can define for us,
our waiting selves, a city at night. From sidewalks
a rocking waltz, mirage
of trapped heads in a blue moving aquarium.
Curious how fast, underwater,
the woman at the front can tap a smoke
from its pack, hand a small white *danseuse*.
Or how quick the autistic boy
lines up pens, end to end.

The bus fusses with itself like a stout man
with indigestion, bloated and hissing
at the curb. When it soaks us in a backdraft
of leaves and grit, we tell ourselves its anger
is aimed at the city itself:
the finite geography of set routes.
The diesel hull of its mind dreams
rutted back roads, burnouts on drag strips.
It wants the view from make-out point,
Cabot Trail. But it knows it's caught—
Main to High to East and back; the locked-
in days, terror-shadows of the station garage.

During strikes it lets its waist go, drinks too much.
But we know it will always arrive
at our stop, idling
with the patience of a monk while we muck
up its insides. There's acceptance
in its stops and starts, the way it never makes
a run for it. Comfortable in the planned life,
gridded in careful direction. And it needs us,

huddled together with
newspapers over our heads,
the only thing it can't quite grasp.
When it comes I push to get in,

office glare aging faces
in this chest of forced daylight—
old slow metal mammoth with scars from across town,
pregnant with our small talk and magazines.

NEXT DOOR DOG

Your call's pantheistic
and coded in the yanked
chain of *Canis* DNA.
Channelling the Pleistocene,
your bay wakes Wepwawet,
Fenrir, slick-hided tricksters
sent to hex my careless
neighbours. No wonder
you're frantic for your elders—
the keen goes all week
with no slack on the leash.
Full disclosure: I did nothing
during the first December wallop.
You stood like a mastodon
wrapped in permafrost,
wailing out the worst of it
until you gave up or out,
fell to a furred coil of
dropped rope, dog outline,
wisp of hair
from a hundred yards—
nothing but curve, lip
snow dune, Brancusi bird.
To atone I'll pray
for the Revelation
when all Canidae rise up
to greet the Dog Star,
praise the feral
and eat the sun.

They filled in Red River and took our forts,
forced the next batch of kid drinkers to ferret
out new hovels. Our town's skin condition's
making inroads past Pine Glen—plots auctioned
off for the dubiously rumoured big-box.
Between visits one more stretch of frames dance
themselves together, the sturdy bones
of pachyderms singing the wind in the slash
off dirt roads. The neighbourhood's on the fence,
indignant but tickled by convenience—
two banks and the Superstore's NB Liquor—
what to do when woods go power centre?
Down fresh cut subdivisions, flat screens
luminesce like deep sea invertebrates.

ELEGY FOR GIL MARTIN

His face ingot and ironwood,
feldspar, stoveweight.

Stewed on rum, he ground through
jokes on cockless slobs and buggery,

couldn't give two fucks
for a funeral—*Burn me*, he'd said,

so that's what they did. We'll mix
him in the grey swells

off the coast of Baie-Sainte-Anne,
watch the stiff arm of drag

flex what's left downstream—
a bloom of ash in the black.

NATURE VERSUS NURTURE

Sinewy hood tweaked by Small Man Syndrome,
he haymade the temples of shy kids who spoke
up, thumped metalwork on the thin tin
of brainpans, his elbows two ball-peens

for heads. One day skinhead, one day street thug,
he'd fight featherweight cage fights then jack up
for higher classes, his skewed knuckles
gunning for the gristle of bigger men.

All this after his old man crumbled in the shower
at our middle school sleepover. One might argue
there's moments the mind goes critical,
the self reaching its Schwartzchild radius:

the covered body brought down the driveway,
his hand puffed up from cuffing drywall,
the skid of blood from a half-landed jab
on the front hall's landing. Though could be he'd

go that route regardless, a predilection
for playing the mouthy hopped-up convict
coded in the backrooms of the genome:
his cells taut with slights before birth.

A HISTORY OF THE BILLIARD BALL

Shirking bills and the kid, he anchors
    the driftwood
        of a drink-puffed body by the baulk end,
considers celluloid balls blowing up from breaks
       to take the hands
of shore-leaved sailors;
considers the feathered carom like the tick of a clock's hand settling

into its own empty-roomed minute; considers
genealogies of density—
        polished dung or wood scooped
           from the bellies of bloated oaks
and sanded to sphere,
        Bakelite and acrylic's crystal lattice;

      considers elephants shaggy with rot,
mowed down by bow-tied poachers after a half bushel of balls
and a handful of ferrules
       for London snooker halls.

He stops mid-shot,

remembers loss
and the chemistry of games—
      the soft cushions of us plasma and salinity
like hearts—
      and hopes for stone, rigidity,

to become the carbon we're all
          melted down to.

MISCUE

Some men outrun the vectors that contain
their shots, some shoot like it's raining.
Some unmanned from a miscue when they bring
a half-chalked tip inches from a light bulb, sing
a song of curses and wait for the next break-
and-run, the next up eyeing the long string,
bisecting slate with a gaze that's pure line,
a looped circuit plotting breadth for the win.

To conjoin, cohere: in the potholed drags of an
opponent's head a wad of ganglia pulse
like mating snakes, map outcomes, wax
Euclidean. The mind's eye's still muscle
memory, the chafe of twenties against
palm all presage, a weak song in the spine,
ticks of faith from the body's Geiger counter
before any shot's taken. Before the miss,
the loss. Set, match, reassurance: still men.

HOW TO SHOOT SKEET WITH MY GRANDFATHER'S LOST DOUBLE BARREL

Be not green at the gills or *gauche*, not gun shy,
not out of time, not of it, but with the universe
and all in it hewed to stance, to lean.

Hold the barrel like a bible's spine,
like the back of a lover's calf, stare down
the sky's off-white and muscle up to the sight.

Amble to the pitch, sway with the wind
like a highwayman at a halfway house.
Smell not rain sky or dog's fur; rather,

smell pipe smoke stilled in the wood grain
that's the breath of huddled kids holding feathers.
Aim: a borehole outside the day's calculus.

Cut a tangent line off the clouds, feel the
disc in its pulled spring trap, artless ashtray,
terracotta dove nested in a bladed hand,

ripe to fall in a blur of Gaussian spread.
Somewhere off sightline, a flightless bird
dies and its bones erode at the bottom

of Belleisle Creek; its wings two triggers
you knuckle with muster and gut. Don't fuss;
say a prayer and yell, *Pull.* There's recoil there

that will remember itself in the butt's wood
for sixty years. Break the action over
an arm; hold frame—a sportsman's *Pietà.*

Make peace with her: polished fossil, drowsy cat,
retooled sailboat, tone-dead echo lost
in the nautilus of your inner ear.

There's an ingrown rhubarb patch around back
of my grandfather's farmhouse: plant the shells
that opened like orchids in the chamber; think

wood and flesh, mulch, pipe tobacco on stone,
crumbled shale, clay targets softening to peat.
It's never loss but a changing of forms.

HORIZONTAL AXIS WIND TURBINE OFF THE SUNRISE TRAIL

Expecting yawp I get whisper,
each blade a house-width of tempered oar
sculling the troposphere,
throbbing shadows on blue spruce and tarmac.
Hard to approach without flinch,
put faith in the finer points
of tensile strength, wind shear and yaw:
all things considered
she won't fall over.

I take stock like a sixth-grader
at a sock hop, think, *Too close. Too much.*
To Victorian scientists, it'd be mistaken
for some cosmic monolith, honed rotor
planted by moonmen to coax
the earth closer to home. Underneath its cyclic *om*,
I'm giddy-eyed, flattened in the chop
by the arms' pull and taunt, egging me on—

here, easy to think we've already saved ourselves,
filed enough sheaves of wattage
to sate the roots, hauled the planet
back to new equilibriums.
Best not to look at the stairwell
locked to its plinth, the bolted-door
submarine and tank gunmetal,
edged growth on the far side of smoothness.

Let's lay down
on the tread-pawed gravel head to head,
pretend it got here by itself eons ago.
Look up, love, forget how most gadgets
are ruined by their seams, places where rust furs.
Try to count the blur, one arm's spin
ladling a day's worth of sigh and moan every half-second,
torquing us somewhere deeper than bone.

DAYS

We drew in the slack rope of our days
and tied the same knots, took up
bar-hopping, jumped ship on
the practicalities, woke to heads
that felt like botched lean-tos: the Sunday
blues, the nightmare of the night
before's half-filled vodka who-
knows spewing fumes and giving
us the gears from the coffee table. Most days
we thought, Never too old,
        no matter how old we are,
        never too old for air guitar,

for dogging chicks, manning the dog days
of summer on decks. Remember
lobbing empties into the hunched
green ogre of your bumper beat
parking lot dumpster? Them's the days,
in small ways. Feels good to say
we've grown up, shed our skins
of the shitshow. Mostly, though,
I'd say we're still the same age. Some days
I still think, Never too old,
        although we probably are,
        never too old for air guitar.

Wind-scribe, smoke-crate, one-show boob tube
caterwauling pipewise. Plate-steel black box
logging the death-screams of draft. Bullish
and non-negotiable, you'll hiss to grey
ash or go all in for swelter, raking face
with your tinder-licked fraught heart. By day
you read Dante and tick through double-thick
matte black while robins pace your rain cap.
You know a thousand names for flame.
If not heady with kindling, then has-been
dustbin dreaming sleekness firebox and baffle
deep: the day you're sold for scrap and curved
to folk art, anatomy of flue flared for chimes,
weathervanes, new ways of calling storm.

Don't get too jazzed on monikers; some things don't click
after the media blitz. How close to divinity, really,
two-faced wayward angel, tetchy changeling? Game-changer
or space-filler, Rube Goldberg rant on a Feynman diagram.
Given the Standard Model, you're anecdote to abyss, demiurge.
Without you, matter's prima materia, a static walk through
on nothing to nothing to nothing. Screw angular momentum,
you play Siddhartha to the quarks, all nil spin and stillness, neutral
and nonjudgmental, rationing mass to the masses, the most artful
of subatomic bits. But not so fast; the catch: right now you're
     rumour,
chitchat, probability bee buzzing through the LHC, the smallest
     needle
in the largest haystack. Give it a year and it could go bust:
not God particle but last picked, theoretical blip, high school hunk
past prime, slurring symmetry breaks and heydays.

LARGE HADRON COLLIDER

To find what Chaos drank.

Teraelectronvolts: dense thimbles of storm.

Charmed by underground lakes.

No black holes were harmed in the making of.

You'll find no water here.

Protons dreaming the infinite lasso.

Concrete-lined, like us.

Hit a sinkhole and it's all light and solder.

Don't bother looking.

Cheesy lyrics like "The light of your love."

Quark-gluon plasma.

While above ground, consider your fillings.

FUTON

Fixed in its ways,
its pose is sag.
Skin and bones
broken clock couch,
spring and stressed
pipe. The room's
crack at slumming
it, dorm room
austerity. A jeer
to stable structure.
After each move,
there's less
to it—fundamental
brackets coughed up
and forgotten
among the dust-ball
dross after we've signed
the "Out Inspection"—
attempts to stay,
to spread
oneself out.
At the last place,
before the bed
came, we kinked our
backs on it, felt
the casing like a third
body through
its skin of cushion
while we towelled
each other with
facecloths, the heat's

throb a horsehair quilt
we didn't want.
We expected give
while we pitched,
its frame a weak raft
riding two a.m.,
loosely fastened
but holding.

TROUBLING STATES

i. Risk Assessment

If sipping drinks
in a wayward tavern
on the headlands
of this scrappy tar sand,
don't eye the locals
giving the waitress
what they can, a wink
and a coin trick, ta da,
a half-assed *ooh la la*.
Watch the cracked jokes
about the bartender's
missing finger
or you'll get a haymaker
to collapse and recap
your nose to a concave
rhomboid. Keep a head's up
while keeping your head
down downing your beer's
stale head. Ignore
the Nordic keg-tosser
cussing his girl
and plan your way
to the germ-burnished door.
Graph your risk matrix:
given the metrics,
you're half-past wrecked,
mired in your seat's
polished stick and miffed.
Move; give it your all, pinball

through knocked stools,
the tomfoolery and shtick
of the deadhead blues
and its sloppy croon.
You're screwed—
the place edged and lipped
and you'll never gain the exit
until you learn the syntax
of the chest-bumper,
the pool hall felt-thumper,
the flophouse swagger
to woo the daughter
of the tavern's owner.

ii. Potter Auditorium, Kenneth C. Rowe Management Building,
Dalhousie University

One more PowerPointed schematic
   to hike the static of our collective headache. The past
  hour a slipped disc in the stiff spine of the week.
The day's ham-fisted and sans-serifed,
     lax with its terms and teetering
    like a drunk in a canoe. To leave this auditorium,
   its memorandums, put a moratorium on
the background buzz of an air conditioner's chuff, duck
      out and nix the debrief, deep breathe the air
    clean of screen or Systems Theory. According to
   doctor who-knows-who, things, being what they are,
       are more complicated than they seem. No shit,
now toss me a jimmy to uncork the keystone bolt of this PoMo
          dolt-house—we'll
   unspool the geometry,
      sight-read the falling over and sing it back
in bullet point: the implosion, right angles gone acute,
        glass shards like small birds.

iii. Mask

In grade four I'd try hard to miss the game,
fake sick or throw a fit to jump ship on the team,
while away the night while the mosquito league
adjusted cups, mucked up Tim's uniforms,
fought pop-flys and made cleat cuneiform.
There's victory ice cream but give me Lego, TV,
free reign for garage light pageantry
where I'd flip my bike to make a spoke guillotine
to lop the head off Emperor Palpatine.
Until I quit it was left field on Tuesdays,
mitt over face—a Boba Fett getup—
sunlight and dead stars squared through the webbing.

iv. Muons

Sit a minute
(you were
thinking
of slammed
doors,
how she left):
ten thousand
brushstrokes
just streamed
through
the soft
slow broth
of you,
boring for
deeper waters
before blinking
out.

ABOUT THE AUTHOR

Danny Jacobs grew up in Riverview, NB. His poems have been published in a variety of journals across Canada. After living in a number of cities and towns in the Maritimes, Danny is back in Riverview and works as the librarian in the village of Petitcodiac, NB. This is his first book.

PHOTO CREDIT: SARAH CAISSIE